Oxford First Science Dictionary

Compiled by Graham Peacock

Illustrated by David Semple

OXFORD
UNIVERSITY PRESS

My name is

OXFORD
UNIVERSITY PRESS

Great Clarendon Street, Oxford OX2 6DP

Oxford University Press is a department of the University of Oxford.
It furthers the University's objective of excellence in research, scholarship,
and education by publishing worldwide in

Oxford New York

Auckland Bangkok Buenos Aires Cape Town Chennai
Dar es Salaam Delhi Hong Kong Istanbul Karachi Kolkata
Kuala Lumpur Madrid Melbourne Mexico City Mumbai Nairobi
São Paulo Shanghai Taipei Tokyo Toronto

Oxford is a registered trade mark of Oxford University Press
in the UK and in certain other countries

Text © Copyright Graham Peacock 2003
Illustrations © Copyright Oxford University Press 2003
Illustrated by David Semple
The moral rights of the author/illustrator have been asserted

Database right Oxford University Press (maker)

British Library Cataloguing in Publication Data available

ISBN 0–19–910914–1 Hardback
ISBN 0–19–910915–X Paperback

1 3 5 7 9 10 8 6 4 2

Typeset in Gill Sans MT Schoolbook
by Perry Tate Design
Printed in Italy

Contents

Introduction

The **Oxford First Science Dictionary** contains over 300 scientific words in alphabetical order, each with a simple meaning. Colourful pictures and diagrams support the text, while captions and labels expand or further explain the word.

The words in the dictionary have been carefully chosen to help children develop their scientific language and understanding. At the end there is also a list of science doing words that children are likely to use in their science lessons.

position of letter in the alphabet

alphabet

capital letter

small letter

beginning letter

word

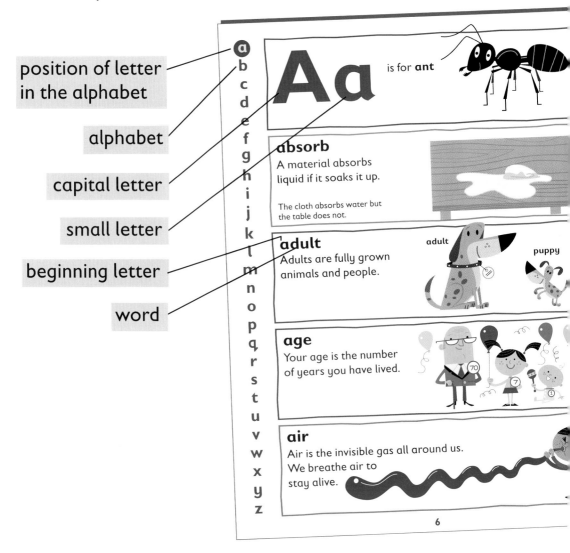

a b c d e f g h i j k l m n o p q r s t u v w x y z

Aa

is for **ant**

absorb
A material absorbs liquid if it soaks it up.

The cloth absorbs water but the table does not.

adult
Adults are fully grown animals and people.

adult

puppy

age
Your age is the number of years you have lived.

air
Air is the invisible gas all around us. We breathe air to stay alive.

6

The dictionary will also teach children how to locate a word using its first letter, and how to interpret information from words, pictures, and diagrams.

Finally it will foster children's natural curiosity about living things, everyday materials, and physical processes.

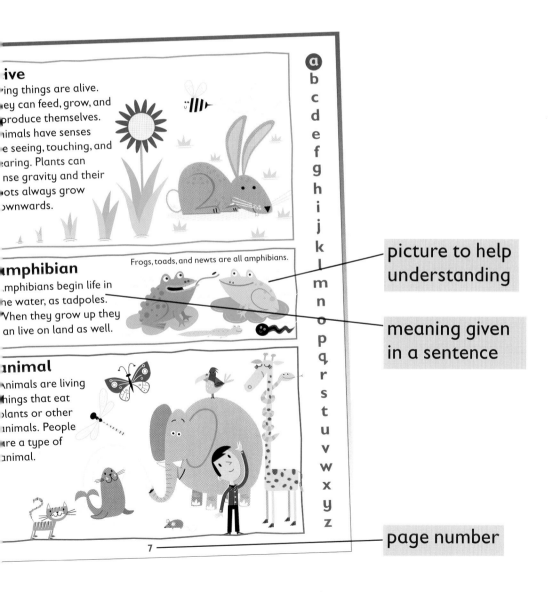

ive
ring things are alive.
ey can feed, grow, and
produce themselves.
nimals have senses
e seeing, touching, and
aring. Plants can
nse gravity and their
ots always grow
ownwards.

mphibian
Frogs, toads, and newts are all amphibians.
mphibians begin life in
ne water, as tadpoles.
When they grow up they
an live on land as well.

animal
Animals are living
things that eat
plants or other
animals. People
are a type of
animal.

a b c d e f g h i j k l m n o p q r s t u v w x y z

picture to help understanding

meaning given in a sentence

page number

7

Aa

is for **ant**

absorb

A material absorbs liquid if it soaks it up.

The cloth absorbs water but the table does not.

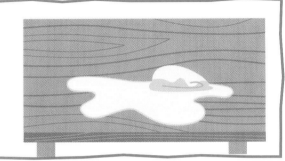

adult

Adults are fully grown animals and people.

adult

puppy

age

Your age is the number of years you have lived.

air

Air is the invisible gas all around us. We breathe air to stay alive.

alive

Living things are alive. They can feed, grow, and reproduce themselves. Animals have senses like seeing, touching, and hearing. Plants can sense gravity and their roots always grow downwards.

amphibian

Amphibians begin life in the water, as tadpoles. When they grow up they can live on land as well.

Frogs, toads, and newts are all amphibians.

animal

Animals are living things that eat plants or other animals. People are a type of animal.

a b c d e f g h i j k l m n o p q r s t u v w x y z

a
b
c
d
e
f
g
h
i
j
k
l
m
n
o
p
q
r
s
t
u
v
w
x
y
z

ankle

Your ankle is where your foot joins your leg. Ankles are joints.

ankle

antenna

An antenna is a feeler on the head of some tiny animals. The plural of antenna is antennae.

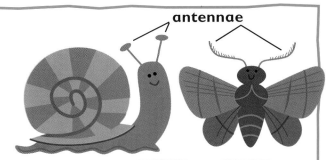

antennae

antibiotic

Antibiotics are drugs. They cure illnesses caused by bacteria (tiny germs).

antibiotic

arm

Animals that walk on two legs have arms at the top of their body.

asthma

Asthma is an illness that makes it difficult to breathe.

An inhaler helps someone with asthma to breathe.

attract

If one object is pulled towards another we say it is attracted.

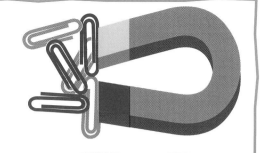

A magnet attracts iron and steel objects.

Bb is for **bat**

baby

A baby is a young animal.

A baby hen is a chick and a baby horse is a foal.

back

You can feel your backbone. It runs down the middle of your back.

Backs bend both ways.

bake

When you bake food you heat it in an oven.

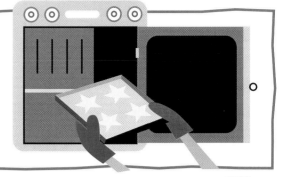

Food changes when it is baked.

battery

Batteries store electricity.

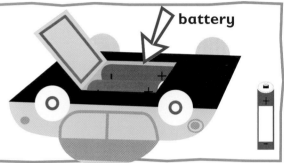

battery

beak

A bird's beak is its mouth

The shape of a bird's beak depends on what it eats.

berry

Berries are small, round, juicy fruits.

bird

Birds are animals with feathers, wings, and a beak.

Ostriches are the largest birds, hummingbirds are the smallest.

hummingbird

ostrich

parrot

blackbird

birth

At birth a baby comes out of its mother's body. Mammals give birth to babies. Most other animals hatch from eggs.

A whale mother gives birth under water.
She pushes the baby to the surface to breathe.

blind

Blind people and animals cannot see.

The guide dog sees for its owner.

blood

Blood is a red liquid that takes food and oxygen to all parts of the body.

When you cut yourself, blood leaks out. But it soon goes hard and forms a scab.

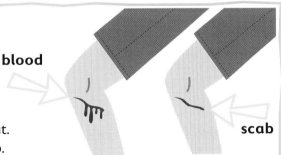

blood

scab

body

The body is all the parts of an animal.

Some animals' bodies have legs but some don't.

a
b
c
d
e
f
g
h
i
j
k
l
m
n
o
p
q
r
s
t
u
v
w
x
y
z

a
b
c
d
e
f
g
h
i
j
k
l
m
n
o
p
q
r
s
t
u
v
w
x
y
z

boil

Liquids bubble when they boil.

You have to heat a liquid to make it boil.

bones

Bones make the hard frame of our body. Most skeletons are made of bone.

Bones show up on X-rays.

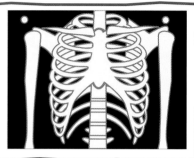

brain

Brains control thinking and movement.

Patch – dinner!

bubble

Bubbles are little pockets of gas in a liquid.

The outside of a soap bubble is a thin layer of liquid.

bud

Buds are flowers or leaves that have not opened yet.

Inside a bud the leaf or flower is tightly folded.

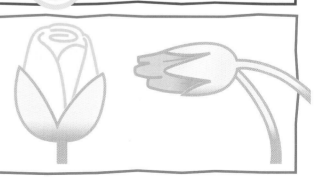

bulb

Light bulbs glow when electricity passes through them.

The glowing wire in a light bulb is called the filament.

burn

When an object burns it gives off heat. Flames rise from burning things.

bush

A bush is a woody plant. It does not have a tall trunk like a tree.

bush   tree

buzzer

A buzzer makes a sound when it is in a complete electric circuit.

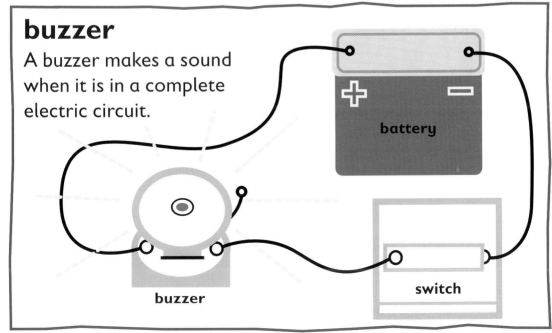

battery

buzzer   switch

Cc is for crocodile

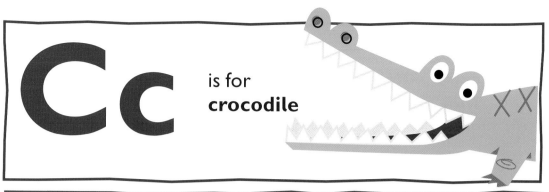

cactus

Cacti are desert plants. They have swollen green stems, and spines instead of leaves.

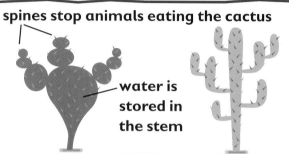

spines stop animals eating the cactus

water is stored in the stem

camera

A camera is for taking pictures. It has a lens to let in light. The light makes a picture on the film.

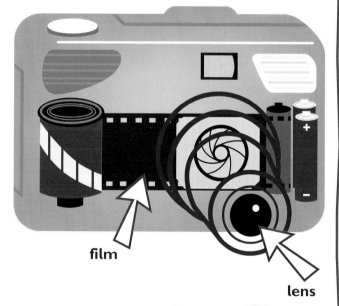

film

lens

camouflage

A camouflaged animal is one that blends in with its background.

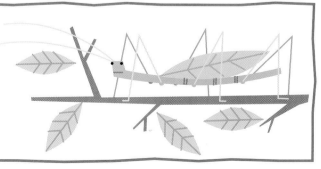

Spot the camouflaged animal.

14

carnivore

Carnivores are animals that eat other animals.

What do these carnivores eat?

caterpillar

Caterpillars look like worms with legs. They are a stage in the life cycle of many insects.

Caterpillars are a type of larva.

cereal

Cereals are food plants such as wheat, rice, oats, and maize. Breakfast cereals are made from these plants.

chemical

Chemicals are substances made in laboratories and factories. They include plastics and medicines.

circuit

Electricity travels round an electrical circuit if there is no break in the wires.

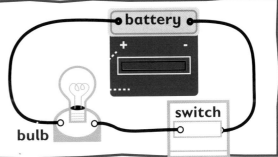

battery

bulb

switch

claw

A claw is a sharp part on the end of an arm or leg.

Many animals have claws on their feet. A crab's pincers are claws.

clay

Clay is dug out of the ground. It can be baked hard to make bricks, tiles, and cups.

cloud

Clouds are made when tiny drops of water form in the air.

coal

Coal is black rock that burns easily. It is made of trees that died millions of years ago.

cocoon

A cocoon is a silk case that a caterpillar spins around itself when it becomes a pupa.

The silk we make into clothes comes from silkworm cocoons.

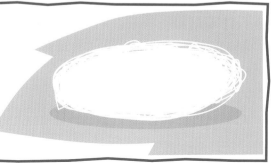

cold

An object is cold when it is at a low temperature.

The drink is cold.
The ice cream is colder.
The ice is even colder.

cold-blooded

A cold-blooded animal has about the same temperature as the air or water around it.

Reptiles sunbathe to warm up their bodies.

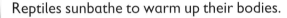

colour

There are millions of colours. We can see colours, but some animals only see in black and white.

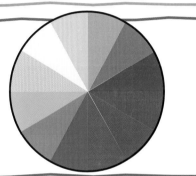

conduct

Materials that let electricity pass through them are called conductors.

The wires in the circuit conduct electricity.

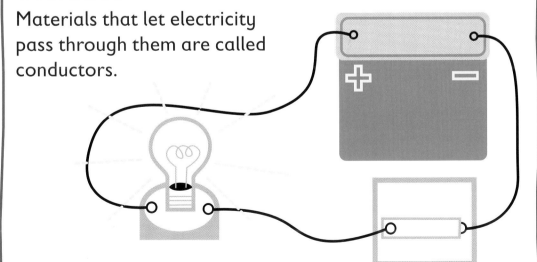

a b **c** d e f g h i j k l m n o p q r s t u v w x y z

a b c d e f g h i j k l m n o p q r s t u v w x y z

cool

To cool an object you drop its temperature. Liquids turn into solids when they are cooled.

When liquid jelly cools, it becomes solid.

crystal

Crystals are rocks such as quartz, salt, and diamond. They have regular shapes. Salt crystals are cube-shaped.

You can grow some crystals in a jar.

Dd   is for **dog**

dark

A place where there is no light is dark.

day

During the day the Sun gives us light. A day can also mean 24 hours.

dead

A living thing is dead when it stops growing, moving, and feeding.

deaf

A deaf person cannot hear sound.

Some deaf people talk using sign language.

decay

When something decays it goes rotten and begins to fall apart.

diamond

Diamond is a type of crystal. It may be dug from deep in the ground.

Diamond is the hardest material there is.

diet

An animal's diet is what it eats. A balanced diet for a person contains many types of food.

cereal

a b c d e f g h i j k l m n o p q r s t u v w x y z

digest

Animals digest food in their stomach and gut.
The food gives them energy and helps them grow.

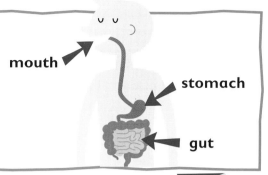

mouth

stomach

gut

dilute

To dilute something you add more water.

Dilute juice does not taste as strong.

water

orange

dinosaur

Dinosaurs were a group of reptiles that died out millions of years ago.

Tyrannosaurus

Triceratops

disease

A disease is an illness. Chickenpox, a cold, flu, and stomach upsets are all diseases.

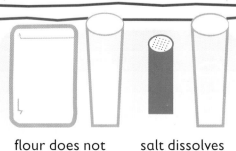

dissolve

When a solid dissolves in a liquid it makes a solution. You can see through a solution.

flour does not dissolve

salt dissolves in water

drug

A drug is a chemical that affects our body. Aspirin is a drug that is used to stop pain. Alcohol is a drug in wine and beer.

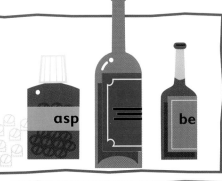

dust

Dust is small specks that float in the air. When they fall they make objects dusty.

In countries where there is little rain there are sometimes dust storms.

Ee

is for **elephant**

ear

You hear sounds with your ears.

Ears come in all shapes and sizes.

Earth

The planet we live on is called Earth. Another name for soil is earth.

The Earth is a huge ball of rock.

a b c **d** **e** f g h i j k l m n o p q r s t u v w x y z

echo

An echo is a sound that has bounced back from a wall.

It takes time for the sound to travel to the wall and back.

egg

Eggs are the starting point for a new animal. Birds lay eggs with hard shells. Crocodiles lay eggs with leathery shells. Frogs lay masses of eggs in jelly.

elastic

Elastic materials spring back into their original shape.

elbow

Your elbow is the joint between your upper arm and your lower arm.

elbow

Elbows work like hinges on a door — they don't twist.

electricity

Electricity is a flow of energy.
It usually comes from a battery or from the mains.

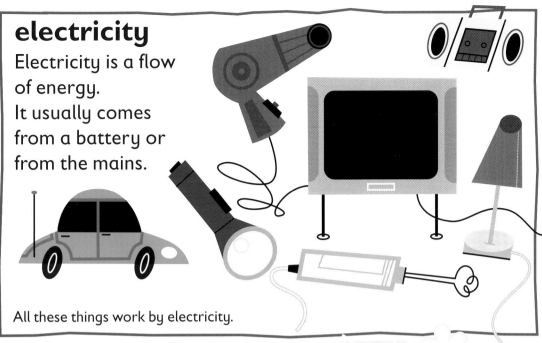

All these things work by electricity.

energy

Energy is the ability to do work. This could be lifting, carrying, or heating something.

engine

Engines are machines that can move things. Engines need fuel such as petrol, diesel, or coal to work.

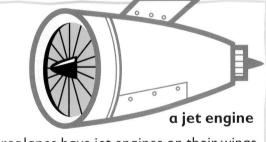

a jet engine

Aeroplanes have jet engines on their wings

evaporate

When a liquid evaporates it changes into a gas. Evaporation happens more quickly if the air is warm.

We want water to evaporate from wet washing.

a
b
c
d
e
f
g
h
i
j
k
l
m
n
o
p
q
r
s
t
u
v
w
x
y
z

a b c d e f g h i j k l m n o p q r s t u v w x y z

exercise

People and other animals need exercise to keep fit and healthy.

experiment

When you experiment you try something out and see what happens.

How do you think this experiment will end?

extinct

When a type of animal or plant is extinct, none are left alive.

The dodo is an extinct bird.

eye

You see things with your eyes.

Some animals have large eyes to help them see at night.

24

Ff

is for **frog**

face

Your face is the front part of your head.

The faces of people, chimps, gorillas, and monkeys have things in common.

fat

Many foods contain fat. Cheese and butter have lots of fat. Vegetables and fruit have only a little fat.

These are all high-fat foods.

feather

Birds have feathers. No other animals have them.

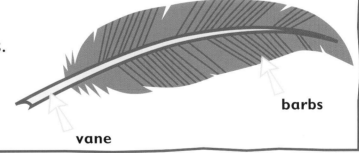

barbs

vane

feed

Animals feed on plants or other animals.

female

Female animals give birth to babies, or lay eggs. They usually look after the young.

fin

A fish flaps its fins to help it swim.

dorsal fin

tail fin

pectoral fin

finger

You have four fingers and a thumb on each hand. They are good for gripping.

The nails at the end protect the fingertips.

fire

To start a fire, you need fuel, air, and heat.

Putting water onto a fire will put it out.

fish

A fish is an animal that lives in water and breathes through gills.

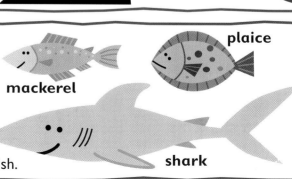

plaice

mackerel

shark

There are many different types of fish.

flame

Flames are produced when a fire is burning.

float

Objects float in water when they are not resting on the bottom.

The ball and the fish are both floating.

flower

Flowers are the parts of a plant that make seeds.

fly

Animals that fly can move through the air for long distances.

Bats, most birds, and many insects can all fly.

fog

Fog is cloud at ground level. You cannot see far in the fog.

Fog is made of tiny water droplets.

a b c d e **f** g h i j k l m n o p q r s t u v w x y z

food

Animals need food for energy and to help them grow. Plants make their own food from water, air, and sunlight.

foot

Some animals have feet at the end of their legs. Others have hooves, paws, or webbed feet at the end of their legs.

force

Forces can be pushes or pulls.

fossil

A fossil is the remains of an animal or plant buried in rocks.

This is the fossil of a fern.

freeze

When a liquid freezes it turns to a solid.

Ice lollies can be made from frozen fruit juice.

friction

Friction is the force that slows down moving objects.

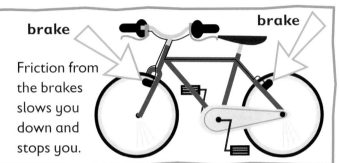

brake

brake

Friction from the brakes slows you down and stops you.

fruit

Fruit is the fleshy part of a plant that covers a seed.

Some fruit has small seeds, other fruit has large stones.

fuel

A fire needs fuel to help it burn. Engines need fuel to make them work.

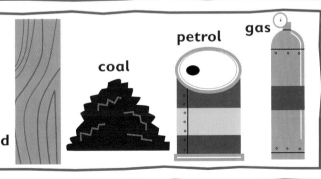

gas

petrol

coal

wood

fungus

Mushrooms and toadstools are types of fungus. They feed on decaying plants or animals.

a b c d e f g h i j k l m n o p q r s t u v w x y z

Gg

is for **goat**

gas

A gas is able to spread out to fill any container. Air is an invisible gas that is all around us.

A bunsen burner burns gas.

germ

Germs are tiny living things that can make us ill.

When you sneeze, germs shoot out of your nose and mouth.

germinate

A germinated seed is one that has begun to grow.

Seeds only need water and warmth to germinate.

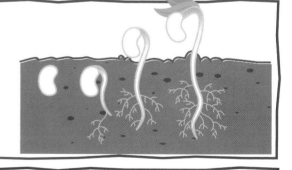

gill

Fish breathe through their gills.

Fish take in water through their mouth and push it out through their gill slits.

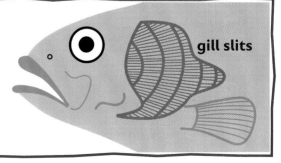

gill slits

glass

Glass is a hard, shiny, see-through material.

Glass can be many different colours.

grass

Grasses are flowering plants that have long, thin leaves.

Bamboo is a type of giant grass.

gravity

The Earth's gravity pulls everything down to the ground.

grow

Living things grow and get larger.

Trees grow and get bigger all their lives.

gut

Your gut is where most of your food is digested.

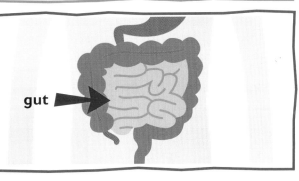

gut

a
b
c
d
e
f
g
h
i
j
k
l
m
n
o
p
q
r
s
t
u
v
w
x
y
z

Hh

is for
hedgehog

habitat

Habitat is the place where an animal or plant lives.

The habitat of these birds is the cliff and seashore.

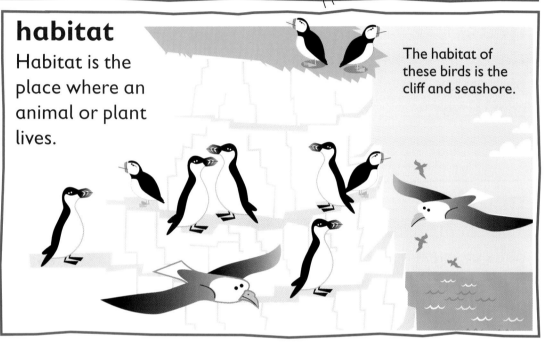

hair

Hairs are thin threads that grow from the skin of many animals. Some plants have hairs, too.

hard

An object that cannot easily be cut or squashed is hard.

All these materials are hard.

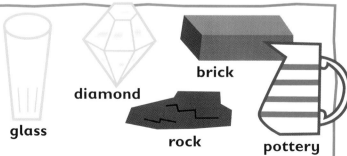

glass

diamond

brick

rock

pottery

head

The head is the part of the body at the top or front.

Most animals have their brains, eyes, ears, and mouth in their heads.

healthy

A person, animal, or plant is healthy if their body is working well.

heart

An animal's heart pumps blood around its body.

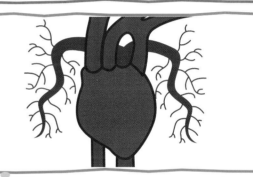

The heart is a muscle that works all the time we are alive.

heat

Heat is a form of energy. Flames give off heat.

The Earth is heated by the Sun.

human

You are a human.

All people are human.

a b c d e f g h i j k l m n o p q r s t u v w x y z

Ii

is for **iguana**

ice

Ice is the solid form of water.

Icicles, snowflakes, and a frozen pond are forms of ice.

incubate

Birds incubate their eggs by keeping them warm with their bodies. Baby mammals have to be kept warm, too.

infect

If you are infected with germs they can make you ill.

This boy is infected with chickenpox germs.

insect

An insect is an animal with six legs.

All insects have three parts to their body.

insulate

If you insulate a hot object you keep it warm.

You can use a flask to insulate a hot liquid from the cold air.

J j

is for **jellyfish**

jaw

The bones around the mouth are the jaw.

upper jaw

lower jaw

Teeth are fixed into the jaw bones.

joint

A joint is a place where two bones are joined together.

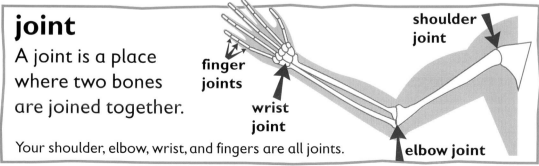

shoulder joint

finger joints

wrist joint

elbow joint

Your shoulder, elbow, wrist, and fingers are all joints.

a b c d e f g h i j k l m n o p q r s t u v w x y z

K k

is for **kangaroo**

knee

Your knee is the joint between your upper leg and your lower leg.

knee

L l

is for **llama**

larva

A larva is the first stage in the life cycle of many insects. Larvae hatch from eggs.

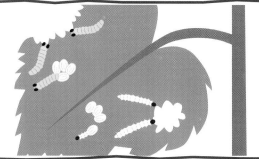

leaf

Plants make food in their leaves.

Most leaves are green.

lice

The small insects that live in people's hair are head lice.

Lice suck blood and make your head itch.

life cycle

A life cycle is made up of the stages of a living thing's life.

The life cycle of a butterfly has four stages.

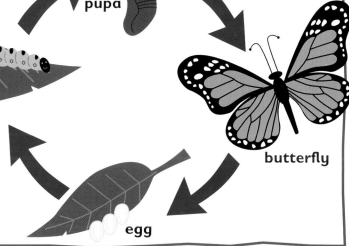

pupa

caterpillar

butterfly

egg

light

Light is a form of energy that we can see with our eyes.

Light comes from many sources.

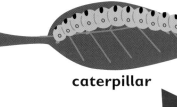

limb

A limb is the arm or leg of an animal.

liquid

Liquids can flow. The surface of a liquid is level.

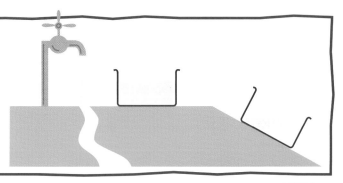

lungs

Many animals breathe air through lungs. Some tiny animals, such as insects, do not have lungs.

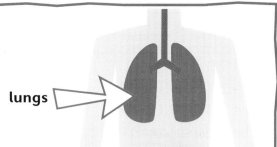

lungs

Mm

is for **mole**

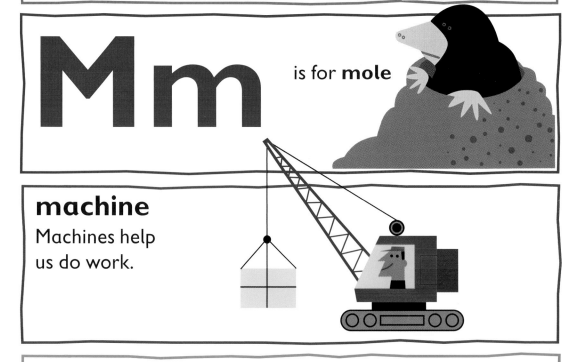

machine

Machines help us do work.

magnet

Magnets attract iron and steel. Two magnets can attract or repel each other.

like poles repel

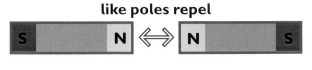

S   N   ⟷   N   S

S   N   ⟩⟨   S   N

unlike poles attract

38

magnify

When a small object is magnified it looks bigger.

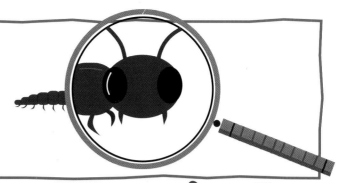

male

Male animals fertilize the female's eggs.

The cockerel fertilizes the hen's eggs.

mammal

Mammals are furry or hairy animals. Mammal mothers feed their young on their milk.

manufactured

Things that are made in factories are manufactured.

These objects are made from plastic or metal, which are both manufactured materials.

material

Material is the stuff that objects are made from.

Cloth, plastic, and wood are all types of material.

a b c d e f g h i j k l **m** n o p q r s t u v w x y z

39

medicine

Drugs that make you better are called medicines.

melt

When solids turn to liquid, they melt.

Solid ice cream melts quickly when it is warm.

metal

Metals are hard, shiny, and cold to the touch.

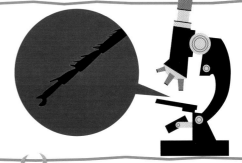

Some metal objects ring when you hit them.

microscope

Looking through a microscope makes really tiny objects look bigger.

Even an insect's legs look big under a microscope.

milk

Young mammals drink milk from their mother's body.

minibeast

Minibeasts are small animals. They do not have bones inside them.

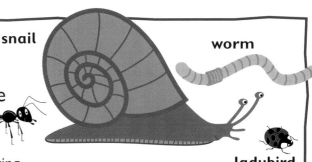
snail
worm
ant
ladybird

Most minibeasts have a hard covering.

mirror

A surface that shows a reflection acts as a mirror.

Many shiny surfaces show reflections.

Moon

The Moon is a rocky ball that goes round the Earth. Other planets have moons going round them, too.

motor

Motors are machines that are used to move objects.

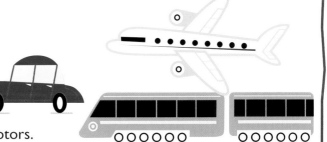

Many forms of transport use motors.

mould

A tiny fungus which grows on other living things is called mould.

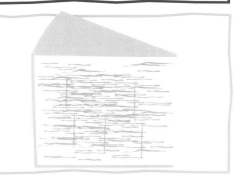

Mouldy foods can be bad for us, but blue cheeses are made mouldy on purpose.

a b c d e f g h i j k l m n o p q r s t u v w x y z

mouth

A mouth is an opening on the head that is used for eating and breathing.

Many animals have teeth in their mouths, and some have long tongues.

muscle

Muscles are parts of your body that pull on your bones so you can move.

Your legs have big muscles.

Nn is for newt

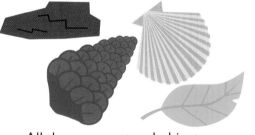

natural

Something is said to be natural if it happens without human help. The plants in a rainforest grow naturally.

All these are natural objects.

neck

A head and body are joined by a neck.

Giraffes have longer necks than zebras so they can eat food from the tree tops.

night

Night is the time when it is dark because the Sun is shining on the other side of the world.

At night, we can see stars far away in space.

non-living

Something that has never been alive is non-living.

Rock, metal, and glass have never been alive.

nose

Many animals have a nose on the front of their head. They use it for smelling.

Rescue dogs can smell people buried under the snow.

Oo is for **octopus**

offspring

Offspring are the young of an animal.

A horse's offspring is called a foal.

a b c d e f g h i j k l m **n** **o** p q r s t u v w x y z

opaque

An object is opaque if you cannot see through it.

Curtains are opaque. You cannot see through them.

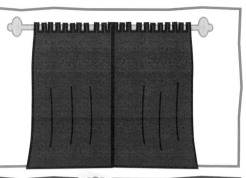

organ

Organs in your body include your brain, heart, lung, stomach, and liver.

Your skin is the largest organ of the body.

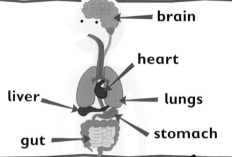

brain

heart

liver

lungs

stomach

gut

oxygen

One of the gases in the air is oxygen.

Animals need oxygen to stay alive.

P p

is for
peacock

paper

Paper is made by mashing up wood with water and squashing it into flat sheets.

We use paper to print on, as kitchen roll, and as toilet paper.

Daily News

parachute

A parachute helps to slow the speed of a falling object.

People and parcels reach the ground safely with parachutes.

paw

Many animals have paws on the ends of their legs.

petal

Petals are the outer part of a flower. They may be brightly coloured.

Some flowers have more petals than others.

plant

Living things that make their food using sunlight are called plants.

Trees, grass, and bushes are types of plant.

plastic

Plastic is a material made from oil.

Plastic can be made into many different shapes.

a
b
c
d
e
f
g
h
i
j
k
l
m
n
o
p
q
r
s
t
u
v
w
x
y
z

a
b
c
d
e
f
g
h
i
j
k
l
m
n
o
p
q
r
s
t
u
v
w
x
y
z

poison

A poison can make you ill or even kill you if you eat or drink it.

There are poisonous chemicals in every home.

pole

The poles of a magnet are at the ends.

The north pole of one magnet attracts the south pole of another magnet.

pollen

Pollen is spread from flower to flower to make new seeds.

Bees take pollen from one flower to another.

powder

A powder is made of tiny grains of dry material.

Sugar and flour are powders.

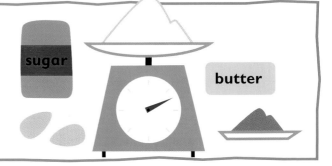

prey

Prey animals are ones that are hunted and eaten by other animals.

The fish is prey for the cat.

pupa

A caterpillar makes a pupa. The caterpillar rests inside the pupa as it changes into a flying insect.

A butterfly pupa is called a chrysalis.

pupil

The dark part of the eye is a hole called the pupil.

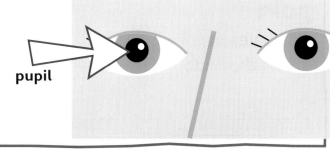

pupil

The pupil lets light into the eye.

pus

Pus is a thick yellow liquid that forms in infected cuts and spots.

Qq

is for **quetzal**

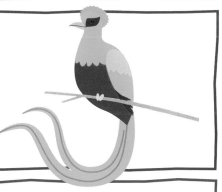

queen

Insects that live in big groups, such as ants and bees, have queens. The queen lays all the eggs.

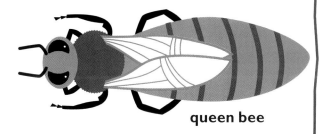

queen bee

a b c d e f g h i j k l m n o p q r s t u v w x y z

R r   is for **rabbit**

rain

Rain is drops of water falling from clouds.

rainbow

Rainbows form when sunlight shines through raindrops.

Sunlight is split into many colours when it shines through drops of water.

reflect

Shiny objects reflect light.

repel

Magnets repel when they push each other away.

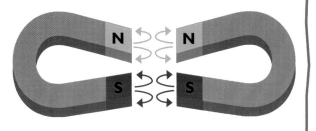

reproduce

Living things reproduce when they have babies, or make seeds that grow, or lay eggs that hatch.

reptile

Reptiles are animals with dry scaly skin. They lay eggs with leathery shells.

Crocodiles and snakes are both reptiles.

rib

Ribs are the bones protecting your chest.

ribs

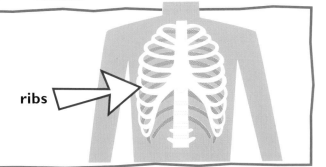

rock

The Earth is made of hard rock.

root

Roots anchor plants in the ground. Plants take in water through their roots.

turnip   onion   carrot

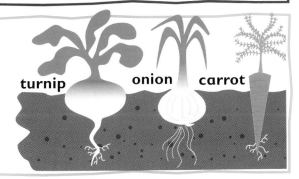

We eat some plant roots.

a b c d e f g h i j k l m n o p q **r** s t u v w x y z

rust

When iron rusts, it gets a reddish-brown covering.

Water and air cause iron to rust.

S s

is for **swan**

salt

Salt is powdered rock that we sprinkle on food.

salt

Salt is also put on roads in winter, to melt the snow and ice.

season

In Europe the four seasons are winter, spring, summer and autumn.

Hot countries may only have dry and wet seasons.

seed

Seeds are dry objects from which a new flowering plant will sprout.

These seeds will grow into new sunflowers.

seedling

The tiny plant that grows after a seed has sprouted is a seedling.

senses

Our five senses are sight, hearing, touch, smell, and taste.

sight

touch

hearing

smell

taste

sex

The two sexes are male and female.

In many birds the male is more colourful.

shadow

The dark area where light is blocked is a shadow.

shell

Shells are the hard outer coverings of snails and some sea animals.

a b c d e f g h i j k l m n o p q r **s** t u v w x y z

a
b
c
d
e
f
g
h
i
j
k
l
m
n
o
p
q
r
s
t
u
v
w
x
y
z

silhouette

A strong shadow made by an object is called a silhouette.

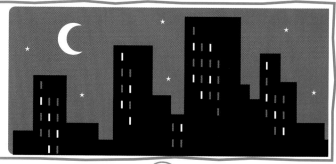

skeleton

A skeleton is a frame for the soft parts of the body.

Your skeleton looks like this.

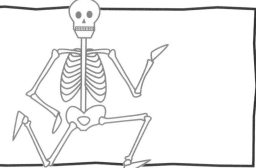

skin

Skin is the body's outer covering.

Many rhinoceroses have very thick, folded skin.

skull

The skull is the hard case of bone that protects the brain.

Many animals have a skull.

horse skull

human skull

snow

Snow is frozen water crystals.

soil

Soil is a mixture of ground up rock and the remains of dead plants and animals.

solid

Solid objects keep their shape. Solids can be cut and joined.

These are all solid.

sort

When you sort a set of objects you put them in groups.

sound

Sound is caused by vibrations. You hear sound with your ears.

When you hit a drum it vibrates and makes a sound.

star

Stars are suns that are so far away they look like tiny points of light in the night sky.

The Sun is our closest star.

stem

The stem is the stiff part of a plant which holds the leaves.

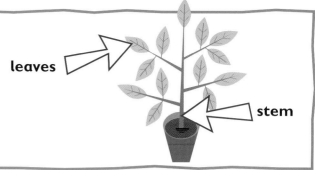

leaves

stem

stomach

Your stomach is the bag into which food goes after you have swallowed it.

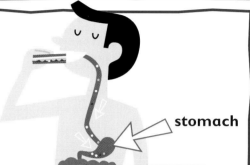

stomach

stretch

When an object is pulled and gets longer it is stretched.

strong

Objects which cannot be broken easily are strong.

The bridge is strong enough to carry the elephant.

Sun

The Sun is a huge ball of burning gas. It gives us light and heat.

sweat

Sweat is the water which leaks out of your skin when you are hot.

Sweat cools you down after you have been running.

switch

A switch can turn electricity on and off.

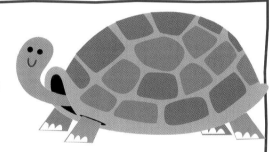

bulb

battery

switch

When the switch is off the circuit does not work.

Tt is for tortoise

tears

Tears are water which leaks out of your eyes when you are sad or in pain.

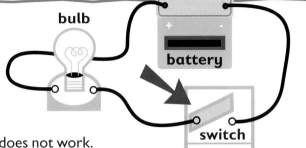

Some people cry when they are very happy!

teeth

Teeth are the hard parts in a mouth which are used to chew food.

Lions have big teeth to hold on to their prey.

a b c d e f g h i j k l m n o p q r **s** **t** u v w x y z

telescope

Telescopes are long tubes with special magnifying glasses at each end.

Telescopes make faraway objects seem much nearer.

temperature

Temperature is a measure of how hot something is.

textile

Textile is another word for a fabric.

One of these fabrics is knitted. The other is woven.

knitted

woven

throat

Your throat connects your mouth to your stomach and lungs.

mouth →

← throat

lungs →

→ stomach

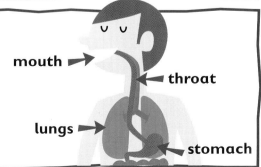

transparent

Transparent objects are see-through.

tree

Trees are large woody plants with a trunk.

Evergreen trees keep their leaves all year round. Deciduous trees lose their leaves in winter.

trunk

trunk

tummy

Your tummy is under your chest. Another word for tummy is abdomen.

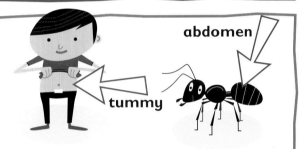

abdomen

tummy

An insect's abdomen is the end part of its body

Uu

is for **umbrella bird**

urine

Urine is the waste water we pass out of our bodies.

V v

is for **vulture**

vein

Veins carry blood around the body.

vein

Veins look blue.

vibration

When an object vibrates it goes quickly backwards and forwards.

volume

Very noisy things have a high sound volume.

W w

is for **walrus**

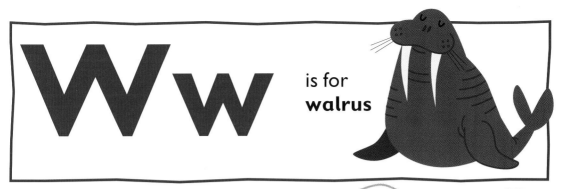

warm-blooded

Birds and mammals are warm-blooded. They keep their body warmer than the air around them.

Hair or feathers help mammals and birds to keep warm.

water

Water is a liquid. It is essential for all living things.

Water can be in solid, liquid, or gas form.

ice

liquid

steam

waterproof

Waterproof materials do not let water through them.

weed

Weeds are plants that we don't want.

Nettles and dandelions are common weeds.

a b c d e f g h i j k l m n o p q r s t u v w x y z

weight

Weight is how heavy something is. To find the weight of an object you put it on some scales.

wing

Wings help an animal to fly.

Aeroplanes have wings to help them fly.

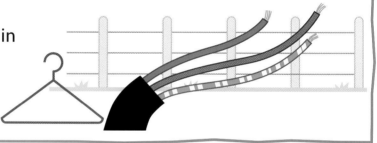

wire

Wires are long thin strands of metal.

Wire is used to make many things.

X x

is for **X-ray**

X-ray

X-rays are invisible rays that can pass through flesh but not bone.
We use X-rays to take pictures of broken bones.

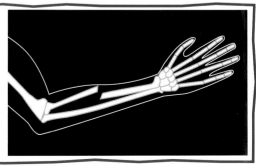

Y y

is for **yak**

yolk

The yolk is the yellow part of an egg. It is a food store for the chick.

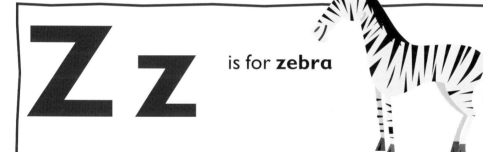

Z z

is for **zebra**

zoo

A zoo is a place where many animals are kept.

Science equipment

computer
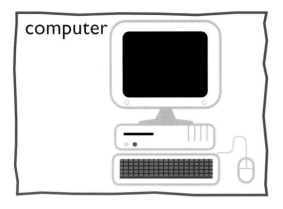

measuring jugs
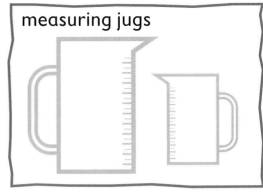

electrical equipment
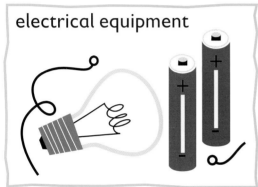

microscope
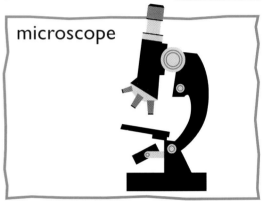

magnets
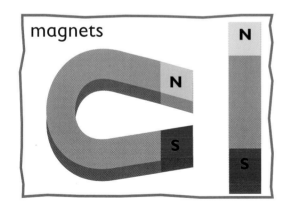

pooter
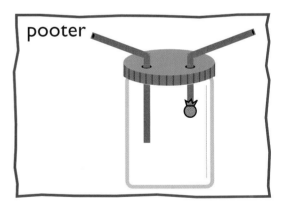

magnifying glass
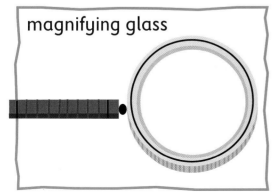

sieves, filters, and funnels
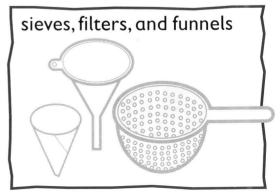

specimen bottle

thermometers

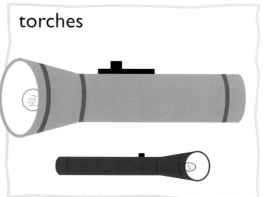

spring balance

torches

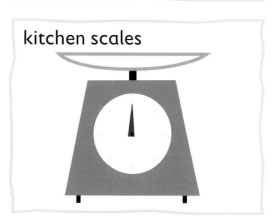

stopwatch

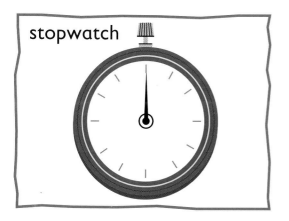

kitchen scales

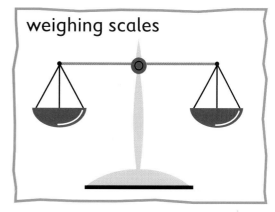

tape measure, metre rule, ruler

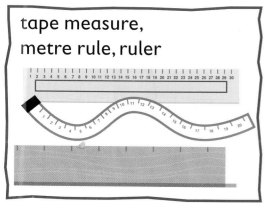

weighing scales

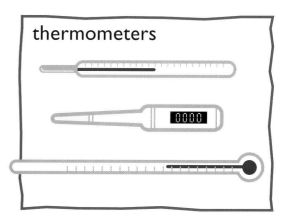

Science doing words

boil
burn
change
classify
collect
compare
cool
count
dissolve
draw
experiment
explain

feel
filter
freeze
graph
grow
guess
hear
heat
listen
look
measure
melt

mix
observe
plan
predict
record
repeat
sieve
smell
sort
test
touch
weigh

flour